Reupholstered Psalms

Reupholstered Psalms

Ancient Songs Sung New

Greg Kennedy SJ
Artwork by Lorraine Roy

Cover design: Troy Cunningham
Cover and interior artwork: Lorraine Roy Art Textiles – www.LroyArt.com;
photographed by Janusz Wrobel
Layout: Audrey Wells

Published by Novalis

Publishing Office
1 Eglinton Avenue East, Suite 800
Toronto, Ontario, Canada
M4P 3A1
www.novalis.ca

Head Office
4475 Frontenac Street
Montréal, Québec, Canada
H2H 2S2

Cataloguing in Publication is available from Library and Archives Canada
ISBN: 978-2-89688-682-1

Published in the United States by
TWENTY-THIRD PUBLICATIONS
One Montauk Avenue, Suite 200
New London, CT 06320
(860) 437-3012 or (800) 321-0411
www.twentythirdpublications.com
ISBN: 978-1-62785-529-7

Printed in Canada.

We acknowledge the support of the Government of Canada.

5 4 3 2 1   24   23   22   21   20

MIX
Paper from
responsible sources
FSC® C103567

For Des and Sandy,
whose love for Earth
has helped me keep the faith

Contents

Starry Night

Introduction

If you are looking for a particular, raw, emotive response to reality and can't find it in the ancient psalms of the Hebrew Bible, then you probably won't find it anywhere. The psalter—that long-established collection of 150 poetic pieces of divinely aimed straight-talk—is a clearing house of emotions arising from all manner of collisions with and celebrations of the human condition, tied inextricably, so claim the Scriptures, to the image of God. Everything you want (and also would rather avoid) is there: love, hatred, awe, disgust, fear, trust, courage, cowardice, obedience, rebellion, hope, despair, joy, contempt, comfort, challenge, incomprehension, wisdom, betrayal, abandonment and communion. I have yet to discover a sentiment in me that wasn't anticipated eons ago in the heart of the psalmist.

This is not to make the ludicrous claim that the world is now what it was 2,500 years ago. Obviously not. So turbulent have been its revolutions—agricultural, scientific, industrial, green, digital and, hopefully very soon, ecological—that an ancient Israelite would feel more lost in the wilds of modernity than she did in the deserts beyond the Red Sea. Likewise, the images, understandings and realities of yore seem at best only remotely familiar to us "uber"-urbanized moderns. The sheep, citadels, swords, chariots, vineyards, customs, political alliances and technologies alive in the psalms can appear mere dead letters to our screen-bred eyes. While timeless in their insight and honesty, the psalms also stand, perhaps demand, to be renovated by each succeeding generation, using the everyday stuff of the contemporary world to allow their deepest possible reach into the soul and psyche of each reader, uniquely placed in the curiosity shop of history.

What follows is my effort to pray these classic and perennial prayers in a context far removed from ancient Israel. Although the emotions and aspirations remain the same, the actors have changed. Now climate change, forced migration, extinction of species, eco-anxiety, consumerism, terrorism and intolerance are the enemies from whom the modern psalmist must plead deliverance. Now God is encountered more often on the city street or the forest trail than in the Temple sanctuary.

The book attempts to restore to today's faithful reader, who has lived victory and defeat in her relation with the divine, the authenticity and rawness inherent to the ancient psalms. It does so to make as real and resonant as possible this relation that took root millennia ago and continues evolving within every person living in a certain time and place. Ultimately, these renovated psalms seek to touch God's presence in the joys and jabs of the life of a believer who is both buffeted and buoyed by the early 21st century.

Such a renovation is best understood as reupholstery. When the fabric of a favourite armchair can no longer contain its stuffing, when the wear and tear already shown starts preventing you from sitting down for fear of inflicting more damage, then the time has come to replace the covering. But just the covering. Reupholstery always retains the frame, because the bones of the furniture in question remain strong. Replacing them would move us into the realm of carpentry, which requires an entirely different set of skills. Carpentry doesn't interest me. First, it isn't needed. The bones of the psalms are as solid today as ever. Second, once we start tinkering with the skeleton of a well-built chair, we run the risk of rendering it unserviceable. Chairs serve a standard purpose, and if you alter their size or shape too much, few people will be inclined to take a seat. They become uncomfortable conversation pieces, more or less useless.

That said, new upholstery can sometimes render a familiar piece almost unrecognizable. Some readers may accuse me not only of poor carpentry, but even of irreverent demolition. I hope that careful and repeated reading will clear me of these charges. In fact, I took my reupholstering very seriously: that is to say, prayerfully. Having studied the skeleton of the original, trying to feel the structural emotions that gave it its form and sturdiness, I then would contemplate the material of our modern world to see what best would cover that abiding, affective framework today. However hard you may find it to believe, I was not at all arbitrary in my rewritings. Not only do I consider that I stayed true to the structural expressions of feeling in the originals, but I would go so far as to say that my reupholstery has granted them new, serviceable lives by updating their colour, texture and style.

The reader can and should test these statements by first taking up the original psalm and then sitting with my reupholstered version. Apart from a couple of obvious variances, the numbers appearing in this book correspond to those found in Roman Catholic bibles to enumerate the canonical psalms. This volume presents the first fifty. Reading the old and the new in tandem will bring out what I would call my fidelity to the former. It will also make the latter a good deal more comprehensible. Not that I fear my renditions will collapse if forced to stand alone. They are much stronger, however, when left leaning on the originals.

While tradition holds King David as their author, no self-respecting biblical scholar ascribes to him the full canon of the psalms. Yet their ancient composers were keen to sign his name to them. This famous attribution lent the psalms credibility. Their real authors experienced no compunction in writing in a voice not their own, in allowing their own emotive response to enter into the reality of another. Similarly, I have no remorse for borrowing the perspective of a tree, a butterfly, a refugee, a woman, an oppressed minority. I feel no need to apologize for taking such poetic licence, for the tradition of the psalms itself grants it.

"Anthropocene" is the term scientists coined to designate our modern reality: that the largest geographical, evolutionary force on the planet today is human. We are the main drivers of extinction, glacial recession, desertification, mineral transformation, material transportation, atmospheric constitution, chemical composition of water, the instability and migration of human and nonhuman populations, and more. We inhabit a world of our making, intentional or not. The Anthropocene is the dark colour of the walls of our present-day living room. Every reflective work of art today must somehow match that interior or look irrelevant and out of place. Although not the typical method of interior design, the following psalms are consciously re-upholstered to set off the wall colour of the Anthropocene. By doing so, they intend to encourage their seated readers to take a better look around.

To the Core #10

∽ Psalm 1 ∽

Happy are those who get happiness,
that is, who understand that God
is on their side. They sit down
together for long hours over tea,
avidly discussing life's blessed minutiae.

14

They are like trees.
Need I say more? Smiling slowly
sunward into a gentle blue eternity
full of fruit and leaves,
reaching a deep kindness
into the heart of Earth.

The ungrateful are not so,
but are like chaff
or, more pointedly, balloons
let slip from a disappointed birthday hand
and blown into steely power lines.
The Lord would love to give them another,
but they can't pry their anguished eyes
from the bit of airy colour trapped
far beyond their grasp.

∾ Psalm 2 ∿

Another pipeline?
One more free-trade deal
to help us haul more easily
every blessed processed thing to market?
All for my own good and warmth and buying power.

Pop the dream we're living in, Lord.
Who can now afford the luxury
of shaking a head in disbelief?
The writing on the walls
of our big box stores and our malls

is not good advertising at all
for the bloody stuff in our carts.

With the same oil once used
for kinging sons
you anoint the Earth,
infirm yet no less royal,
whose reign will not end
although her castle lies in ruins.

You give to those who ask
humbly for the riches of humility.
We're on our knees, all right,
but haven't yet learned to beg.
Distract our pride long enough
to see the splendour of simplicity.
Then with heart in throat sincere
we'll speak happily of our need
of gentle you.

 **Psalm 3**

Mine enemies, who are they?
Who can count them?
As many as the stars
and as hidden by the
torpid lights rising off
the various Babylons that smear
the westernized sky at night.
Theirs is a trimmed-down god,

jealous of his allegiances
and bad choices,
quick to promise paradise
to any wolf, lone or tightly packed,
with teeth enough to tear
a little hell into the flesh
of a highly mediated world.

Lord, I can't tell you what I've
done to draw their hatred.
I suspect they themselves couldn't tell me,
were I to stop and ask them.

On the subway, in the street,
crossing a bridge, inside a café
even beside a mosque disfavoured
I could end up dismembered
simply for passing by.

I'm sick of us and them.
Sick of schoolyard deities
pushing and punching inside a circle
of puerile gawkers
anxious for the red of blood.

Lord, blow your teacher's whistle.
Put the whole stupidity to rest.
Confiscate all the hateful toys
that have been played with
to no good end,
for no one's fun,
least of all your own.

 Psalm 4

Answer me, O God, when I call,
don't let it go to voicemail;
we've connected before
and it was good, I'd say, for both of us.
How much time do we have
to waste ping-ponging messages,
oscillating between two readinesses
to speak that pass like ships
in the night on a sea
populated by more plastic than fish?

O Lord, leave the phone-tag game
to others who don't buy the plan.
But I've always had you
as my provider, you've serviced me
since I had air enough to cry.

When I need to talk
I need to talk,
but the worst is when
the ringtone of that need is silenced.

Lord, you fill me
more than all-you-can-eat sushi.
We've connected before
and it's been good.
Let's not,
neither one of us,
ever forget that.

∽ Psalm 5 ∾

My enemies I've destroyed
with a smile,
a brush of the hand,
a bottle of pills
that readjust delinquent chemicals.

Too harsh is hate,
too hard on the liver;
they've correlated cancer
with negativity;
mean looks cause wrinkles
around the eyes.

I'd rather be in good books
than in bilious newsstand rags.
I won't eat a bite
if the company I've sat down with
gives me indigestion.

Every day I play
tennis on a table
folded up the middle.
My little paddle lobs
the airy, harmless ball
back lightly to itself.

And look! My game doesn't improve;
it's predictable and lonely.

In the absence of my enemies,
in my win (absolutely pyrrhic,
with no one to cheer me on,
or hiss me down)
I've come to question the price
of the *all-good* peace,
the cozy comfort
I purchased
in an impulse pact with the devil.

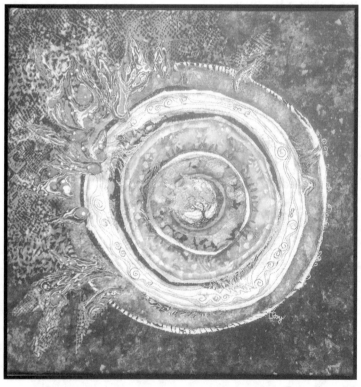

Burning #2

∽ Psalm 6 ∾

One more chemo-beating, Lord,
and I swear I won't get up.
My hope has gone the way
of my hair—lost in chunks,
caught in slimy masses
in the shower drain.
Nothing—not these caps,
not these paisley-printed cloths—
can cover my bald torture.
How long?

Who gets what
from this zombie act
to which I've been so poorly cast?
They're not handing out any Oscars.
Tweak the script, Lord,
and rescue the plunging plot
line of my life.

Spent from sobbing;
smashed in the train wreck
between optimism and evidence;
approaching "Day Zero"
when all my tears will grind
to a dry, dusty halt,
I am the last half-inch
of a cigarette
under a cowboy boot's pointy toe.

Cut out these rebel cells.
Shake the suicidal ideations
out of my bones.
Let us shout aloud together:
    I: *MERCY!*
    You: *VICTORY!*
and we'll watch the tumour,
like the angry tide,
ebb steadily, harmlessly away.

Psalm 7

They would lynch my happiness,
these bleached-white breadcrusts
who have it in for difference.

If ever my pride paraded
down Main Street vaunting
my regal line,
if ever I rubbed their faces
in their own ignorance,
if ever I spat
on their shoes
instead of shined them,
then maybe my innocence
would be a screw or two loose.

But it's plain to see
that the bone of their contention

is the protective coating
my skin was born into.
So wake up, God,
and while you're rightly at it,
give them a good shaking too.

Don't just turn the tables
putting black where white was;
at that point it wouldn't really matter
with supper all over the floor.
Work instead your calmer magic
that stops dead the stupid heckling
with the force of surprising wonder
that suddenly esteems a power
not at all its own.

Let them hit the wall
of their arrogance
and realize it was paper-made.
What's beyond is far better
for all parties concerned:
you, them and folks like me.
Then I'll sing of your justice,
my yesterday blues a new big gospel hymn of praise.

Psalm 8

Boy! What a show!
The first time ever on a farm
at night I looked up
I was like a baby in its crib
captured by the brilliant mobile
fixed above my face
to quiet my isolation.
Then flashed suddenly a city thought:
Those jealous concrete bastards
that swallow up the stars
like cannibal Kronos
in fearful hatred of his children!

When I contemplate the saw-tooth
skyline of sharpened heavenscrapers,
when I see the streets crawling
with sneakered ants and automobiles
I think:
where on Earth aren't we?
what in the World haven't we done?
who drove this square peg home
so forcefully into this round hole?

Yet here we are, little less
than little gods, sneakered and automobiled,
roughhousing the entire family…
and still the darling of creation,
the darling beside billions

of other favourite children—
birds, turtles, lichens,
each longing for a bite
from the apple of your eye!

 **Psalm 9**

Take it all as thanks:
my running sap, my thoughtful buds,
my branching out caught by wind
proclaiming celebration.

Because my enemies have fallen back,
have tripped on the root of our alliance
that turns light to food to breath
to deeper earth made firm
by our vertical covenant.

You reproached the chainsaws
and have made it clear
that naked land devoid of woods
goes against the grain of good.

The cruder desires for emptied
space without the shadow
of any shade you've exposed
as thickly retrograde.

You are national park status
for the groves and copses once overlooked

by western expansion
but now caught in the snaking crosshairs
of the almighty $

Have mercy;
the enemy marches hungry axes
through us, deaf to the counsel
we exude, giving life its upright wisdom.

It's nothing new, but only faster.
Others who felled us
have also fallen into the miseries
of floods, mudslides and lonely, lunar deserts.
They seem somehow provoked
by our happy patience.

Make them climbers not cutters.
Invite them into our upper arms
to share our view of distance.
Open their eyes to us—
both forest and trees at once,
community and individual.
Let them touch our heart
by resting an ear on our bark
and hearing how angels
climb up and down within us.

⌒⌒ Psalm 9/11 ⌒⌒

Why, Lord, do you walk away
refusing to take sides?
Evil has smashed innocence
into innocence and shattered
the glass towers where our safety soundly slept.

Wickedness now is a wasp-nest politics
knocked suddenly out of the tree;
everywhere a furious confusion
stings in the name of divinity's defense.

The great, fanged gears of clockwork war
want turning,
want arms ticking knives
across faithless faces
as they pull in every mobilizing lie
readily at hand.

Who can point to the very mountain
over which this sun insatiable
first slowly rose?
Who can see the ash-heap hill
behind which it will finally set?

Two enemies with guns and pens,
hatefully united by a single genre,
write psalms in blood of ancient loathing;
their compositions contest
exclusive fidelity to the gory text.

You read them, Lord, and weep.
It seems you simply were not made
for this dark red
black-and-white game.

 Psalm 11

Lord, I stick to you
and being stuck
my best I keep trying.
Why then does doubt worm in
and insinuate failure?
Why can't I sit on the porch
and watch the sunset of my deeds
with contented eyes
and a face radiant with colours
borrowed from your sky?

You see through what I do
to what I could;
is the gap really as wide
as I seem to mind?

God, you've got perspective;
you pat the perfectionist head
that instant-replays the entire game
in merciless search for the first
passing shadow of losing
in order to stop the clock
forever there.

28

But you don't really care.
You like the sport
and would rather watch us playing
than see us all huddled up
in the unforgiving need
to score.

∽ Psalm 12 ↶

That good guys finish last, O Lord, is bad enough,
but that they die trampled or shot on the racetrack...
this goes beyond the pale of divine garbage.

Lord, rise up and change the channel:
    the sport is fixed
    the athletes doped
    and the endless ads
    by ruthless sponsors
    could nauseate a maggot.
    Idiotic their lies
    and, worse yet, wickedly lucrative.

God answers:
    *For the losers and for the last
    I cheer, but often you won't hear me;
    I don't bellow or blast horns,
    but my loyalty is rock, immovable.*

Lord, reach in and right the game,
or at least better cheer your team,
for at times the loss feels so great
that your faithful are fit to be tied
to the towel they've listlessly thrown in.

 Psalm 13

How long, Lord, how long
will I grovel for poetry
in this artless life
that reads like the owner's manual
for a vacuum cleaner?

How long will I lose sleep
(that endangered time of dreaming!)
over a serpentine workplace
that has slowly swallowed
the entirety of my geography?

How long will junk mail
and pop-up ads
abuse me with their demeaning
catcalls?
OMG!
on days like these
I feel like the ill-fated squirrel
halfway between tree and peanut

struck on the road
and merged deeper into pavement
with each successive pass
of tires that can't be bothered to swerve.

But all the same,
although pancaked
without an inch of elevation
in my same old, same old,
I trust in you
knowing that your hand,
which holds the peanut out,
will eventually take the other
that grips the wheel.

 **Psalm 14**

Not so much the foolish these days,
but more so the comfortable
murmur distractedly in their hearts,
    There is no God.
It's the price paid for moderate success
that mistakes itself for blinding triumph.

God looks on like a stood-up date,
silent behind the café window,
all those daydreams of summer love
cooling with his neglected coffee.

Better things to do have they;
bigger fish to fry,
and still others more to catch
in a virtual sea of choices.

Sad, really, the entire situation:
God dumped and lonely;
the absent lover caught by the throat
in a chronic, low-level
asthma attack brought on by constant
speed dating.

Most likely the tragedy stems
from this very First-World Problem:
everyone but God has wheels and a cellphone,
which means faith can turn on a dime
away.
The unfortunate formula appears to be this:
the more money spent,
the less time given.
Perhaps the economy will instructively tank
before the relationship totally crashes.

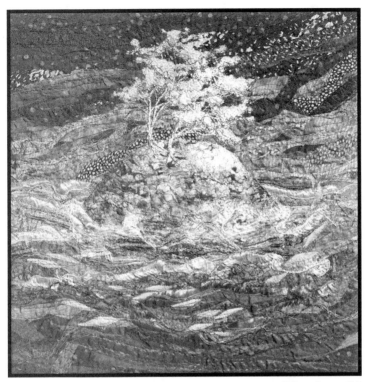

Blessings #1

⌒ **Psalm 15** ⌒

Artist God,
after the flood, be it of water or of fire,
who will come round to your studio?
Who will linger in your gallery?

Those who stand up for beauty
and practise gratitude;
who know truth as community
and sing it in harmony;
who write their lyrics
to the rhythm of other species.

Those who waltz with Earth
instead of slam dance;
who laud you, her poet laureate,
for the rhymes they recite and live by;
those for whom profit is poor motive;
for whom a tree is worth more
standing
than dead and inky in their hands.

Psalm 16

Protect me, my God, like Greenpeace
did the whales,
put your body between my long, soft side
and their explosive harpoons.
The former kicks I got from buying
and driving are gone.
Never again will I worship cars
and blowhard retail outlets.
My lips won't whistle jingles
slyly devised to stick to the roof
of my mind.

Creator, now you are my vehicle
and destination, my store
and my credit card. In you I can spend
myself forever without debt or waste.
With you I party without financial hangover.

You raise my consciousness;
cheap goods now look bad to me,
their thin gold veneer chipped
and showing the rust of rivers poisoned
and the pools of human labour despised.

With you, no more headaches
and consumer withdrawals;
a happy freedom creeps over me,
tickling a laughter I forgot I owned.
Suddenly content with what I have,
I take your joy into my arms.

Psalm 17

Don't listen to me, O Lord.
Don't pay much mind to my ingrown cries,
for often they scream "FIRE!"
when really there's not much more than a touch of heat.

Be more attentive to deeper groans
that struggle up from southern depths
where injustice and innocence
have somehow ill wed into

hurtful stalemates of codependence.
The false positives, the disappeared, the hunted, the hungry,
the abused, the discarded, the polluted, the exploited, the
educated strictly by schoolmasters who teach only out of
their mastery, whole continents scavenging in the garbage
dump of other people's opportunities.
Listen, Lord, listen more to them.
Bend your ear to the twisted grain
of their wooden throats that barely bang out a sound.
Like an old orchard left to mice and deer
they are ravaged, swallowed up by bindweed
and creeping vines;
yet even with their branches barren
you keep them as the apple of your eye.

As for the rest of us,
unsettled by the flow of refugees,
don't let us sew our hearts up tight,
making thus a useless sow's ear
out of an open silk purse.
When the fierce lion of our fears
of losing comforts
paces its cage
roaring at those desperate enough to enter,
please calm its ferocity and clip its claws
for the sake of the weak
far braver than ourselves.
Make us make them brother and sister citizens.
Make them make us match deed to pretty creed.

∾ Psalm 18 ℃

I love you, god creator
of heaven and of earth
for making Me the centre
of all the universe.

My enemies are countless,
they swarm Me like maddened bees,
to name them all is hopeless…
everyone but you and Me;

everyone, because they come
sometime to disagree
with Him alone who's never done
a single stupidity;

everyone, because they come
sometime to disagree
with Him alone who's never dumb;
the sovereign genius: ME!

and you, of course, that's true.
Who could forget the Most High?
I look down to find you
when we don't meet eye to eye.

After all, you made Me
pretty much a god Myself.
Psalm 8 states it clearly.
Yes, I know it very well.

The best thing that's happened
to this old, seven-day earth
is the world that was fashioned
at the moment of My birth.

you've made Me tall, strong and just;
I've never let you down.
Now, between the two of Us,
I'd say I deserve the crown.

you should wear it now and then
like you always did before
so to teach all stupid men
that truly I am Lord!

 Psalm 19

The sky blues
the stars shine
time itself,
when given space,
faithfully conveys day to day
the flowering message of presence.
Talk is cheap;
the real connoisseurs don't buy it.
They afford the silence
that sets like jewels
everything in music.

The sun, splendid groundhog,
hustles out and into her hole—
the lights go on
then off
in this living room world
between ice ages.

The Law of the Lord is perfect
once you find it
working *pro bono*
in the Supreme Court of your heart.

As for the rules,
they're like honey from the comb
once you lose your fear of stings
and get to know the bees.
What I don't see about me
is bad news splashed
across the front page
of other people's papers.
Protect me from my pride
because it's a real brawler
when it staggers out of the bar.

May my words say at least one thing
truly.
May my talk provoke
your famous smile.

Psalm 20

God: wild chamomile green
in the hairline crack between hard places
and unyielding rocks,
God: among the tourists in cathedrals,
God: off the charts kept by health professionals
God: uncorked bottle-genie…
not someone we ever understand
but always invited to our better parties
and, yes, always coming through!

All this now I know for certain,
despite recurrent bouts of early onset
dementia.

Often you see the fast technologists
broken down at the side of the road
where the steady God-walkers
like to stretch their sculpted legs.

God: attentive songbird
wildly vocal
especially now
in mating season.
Give us to sing.

 Psalm 21

Lord, the refugee celebrates your triumph!
In her miserable camp
of scarcity and insecurity
she sings you, often through tears,
hymns of victory.

From a clear graveyard
you've led her to a vague waiting room
you've spared her life but not the
sufferings that make for thrilling
autobiographies of the handful few
who get a chance to write them.
The irrational tenacity
and stranglehold on hope
that marched her through deserts
over oceans and down the throats
of beastly entrepreneurs
were gifts ambiguous granted by your
inscrutable hand.
Scorn, hostility and vengeful bureaucracy
populate her new safe haven
deepening her dependence on You.

Let the comfortable in their comfort consider;
let the propertied ponder impermanence;
let everyone,
the entitled no less than the dispossessed,
gnaw on the bone that we all live but a stone's

throw from the road
and even those sitting armed on their big verandahs
look out anxiously in the distance for a fairer home.

Get them up, Lord, help them
open their white picket fences
and together we'll cheerlead your power!

∽ Psalm 22 ∾

My God, my God, it's all out of my hands!
Is it out of yours too?
When I don't wake up in a cold sweat
from climate nightmares,
I sleepwalk through first-world problems
dimly traumatized by survivor's guilt.

It was simpler once.
People died good or bad
according to the amount of blood on their hands.
But I wash and wash and can't come clean.
In fact, it just gets worse,
because I'm wasting so much water.

You dropped me here
on Peak Civilization—a mountain made
of playing cards sick to death
of crescendo gambling.
You, not I, chose life

in the century of the Fall.
So what are you going to do now:
put out your hand to catch me,
or your foot to trip me faster?

My pride of place I owe to you
on both sides:
the one, warm and glowing with thanks
for the sunrise of rights and freedoms;
the other, dead cold with hubris
in the stony face of human power.
Stuck between a rock and a good place
my mouth is torn by curse and praise.

Around the world the populists pen me in.
Rehashed nationalism booby-traps
the slapdash fences of its forefathers.
The whole scene grows
more intolerably obscene.
Meanwhile my body melts like paraffin
even as its lifespan lengthens.
I've lost count of the bits
of highly advanced baling wire
holding my whole bony shebang together.
It's a modern miracle that costs too much
for me not to complain.

But you, God, you—writer, director, producer,
not to mention casting agent—
how can you just up and leave the set?
There's no story, no movie, no Academy

Award without you.
Yell "ACTION!" right now
because the rolling cameras
are running out of time.

Then you'll see my transformation,
my steady climb to the occasion.
I never wanted this part.
But now that I've got it and can't get out
I'll play to you, to your direction,
your unseen vision of the Whole.
Tell me who and how I'm to be
and together we'll make cinematic history.

Psalm 23

The Lord is my shepherd, I shall not want.
As I lie down on Toronto's concrete,
the smell of green, buried farmland rises up;
at the public fountain where I bathe with pigeons
he freshens some fragments of my soul.

Along sidewalks thick with people he leads me.
Even though I push my found belongings through metaphors
of a different age, I still get the poetry:
his rod and his staff—things I've only seen as a kid on TV—
they strangely comfort me.

A meal is prepared for me by volunteers.
My head, oiled by unwashed hair,

overflows with ideas—
I've got a lot of time to think.

Surely goodness and mercy follow me;
I just hope they catch up soon and more often.
Still, I'm sure I dwell in the house of the Lord,
because sometimes I manage to feel myself at home.

 **Psalm 24**

Earth and all its merchandise
the shelves, the shoppers and staff,
the trademark and the franchise
all belong to a single account.

Who can wade into the future?
Who can weather the climate storm?
Those with hope as a compass,
who do not greenwash their sadness
or minimize their genuine joy:
generations not born together
but working as if one body.

Stores, throw open your doors!
Set free your troubled stock!
Make room for New Economy!

Who is New Economy?
She's supply and demand
harmonized perfectly by Love.

Stores, throw open your doors!
Don't refuse a single customer
to enter and buy into New Economy!

Who is New Economy?
She is compassion
    globalized.
She is life
    inclusive.

Psalm 24/7

All the time
this spring-thaw flow
of novelty
electrified, doped up, on speed
things to do to do to do
the proud tyranny of busy
always open
forever closed-
up in the theatrical heart
performing non-stop
to a blah-blah-blah audience
ignorant of art
but uber-aware of image
monkey mind
in jungle economics
full of feces-fighting politics

digging pits
and falling in themselves
but not to worry
so long as you hurry
emergency response
is at the ready
every single bloody
night and day.

High Tide #1

 Psalm 25

To you, O Lord my God, I lift up my soul;
I lift it up constantly, neurotically
like an obsessive-compulsive who can't
stop washing his hands.
My thirst for affirmation, for praise
is insatiable.
Yes, I lift up my soul demanding
that it be lifted up.

How it happened I cannot say:
how desert seized my loamy soil
turning it to simple sand
through which rains quickly drain
and the barest breeze deeply desiccates.
So little there is in me
for flowing life to hang on to.

Remind me, Lord, when I get
into one of my states,
when solid earth feels
like choppy lakes
over which I'm blown alone
in my canoe away from the shores
of recognition; remind me then
that there is no end
to your compassion.
Sure, I could intone the litany

48

of your goodness, but that's not what this liturgy
needs right now.
Instead, an honest assessment of my worth,
not at all inconsequential,
yet equally (thankfully) not nearly
as inflated as my insecurity pretends.

Take my restless hands
and hold them into knowing
that they are clean enough,
take my thirsty throat
that can't hear what it's saying
and unbend the fishbone praise
it's choking on.
Free my life from the vain pollution
pumped out as harmful by-product
from my hurting little self.
Save us, O God, from childhood defenses.

Psalm 26

Judge me, Lord, dissect me.
Arrange my innards
on the stainless steel table
in neat rows that narrate
the story of their disassembly.

I have not colluded with the proudest species
in its dominating aspirations.

I revile its absolutism,
its crusade against diversity.
Instead, I've fled ever deeper into the woods
in search of your wildest sanctuary
alighting on the last living pillars
of your forest temple.

Lord, how I love the simple land
that simply isn't owned.

Don't lump me in with that predacious lot.
Let no blood bespatter my wings.
Their mindlessness threatens
to take my heart away.

I, for my part, go from flower to bloom
drinking nectar, spreading life,
joyfully keeping up my creative end
of our holy, earthy bargain.

 **Psalm 27**

The Lord is my lucky shirt:
the days I wear him I walk tall.
The Lord is my pair of canes:
my decrepitude will not keep me housebound.

As my shopping list of troubles lengthens
the more the world is thrashed
beneath an extremely weathered sky,

somehow my heart keeps floating
like a seagull, despite ingested plastic,
bobbing placidly atop the scummy surf.

First my dreams were to be a ranger,
then a farmer forgotten in the fields,
now into the woods I go in search
of you, fond tree-climber,
and when I pause to rest a palm
on one of your living, upright wisdoms
I feel your pulse swaying in the upper branches.

Looking up I see connect two holy reachings,
one: leafy green skyward straining,
one: easy blue earthward bending,
and there, over my head,
the covenantal handshake that holds
hope and peace together.
Where is sealed this sacred deal
besides the temple of your forests?
But all her buttresses have flown
beneath the axe; her walls, ever thinner,
totter in the breeze that once found
in her a choir majestic.

Although abandoned by my antecedents,
although commercialized by my kin,
the woods do not withhold their welcome.
When I accept their gilded invitation
to sit and listen, I suddenly wake up
on the pillow of your heart.

Hope is in the trees.
Stir up your senses and be quiet.
Hope is in the trees,
who stand on guard for God.

 Psalm 28

Language is tricky;
so often we say much more than we mean.
Take your title, O Lord, for example.
"Lord":
patriarchal; feudal; hierarchical; chauvinist with undertones
of classism, oppression, exploitation and bellicosity.
But how lovely it lifts off the tongue!
Like a redwing blackbird off a cattail
catching flight, gaining air,
arcing in a sky as open as an empty page
awaiting words knit colourfully together.

Don't hear in my voice the malice
of other tongues—those rusty nails
that end in lockjaw—convinced
of their words' innocence
even when aimed to kill.
They speak Power to Truth
and at the name of Fear
want every knee to bend.

But I say "Lord" and pronounce Freedom;
I say "Lord" and address Compassion;
I say "Lord" and salute Wisdom,
as gentle as the Monarch's black-latticed wing
against the quiet, upholding air.
"Lord" is my four-letter rock,
a sound I have retrieved
from the midden of cutting shards.
It speaks to me so tenderly
that I cannot help but repeat it.

 **Psalm 29**

Sisters, belt it out!
Rattle the windowpanes singing!
Shatter them if you can.

The voice of the Lord like Janis Joplin.
The voice of the Lord like Mercedes Sosa.
The voice of the Lord like Roberta Flack.
The voice of the Lord like Aretha Franklin.
The voice of the Lord like Nina Simone.
The voice of the Lord like Eva Cassidy.

Thunder. Honey. Ocean. Tornado.
Typhoon. Thrush. Blackbird. Rainfall.
Aspen leaves. Timpani. Trumpet. Marden Creek.
Spring peepers. Crickets. Cicadas. Niagara Falls.

The voice of the Lord like deep lungs
releasing gospel.

The Lord sits behind the snare
and high hat
and never lets up
keeping perfect time.

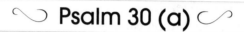 # Psalm 30 (a)

Here's to Freedom!
Here's to the *carpe diem* jailbreak
from the maximum security of Poor Me.
I asked and—holy smokes—got
answers, although not the kind
that fits on Post-it Notes.
After all this faddish matte grey I've lived
inside, I'm going back to velvet flowered wallpaper.

Maybe I have no right to say it right now
when health and food and sanity
all grace my table,
but according to my bird's-eye
all-things-considered calculations,
the good outstrips the bad,
even when the truth is naked.

But there have been times less sanguine,
more heady when I've walked around

my conviction kicking tires,
sure that I had a techno-fix
for this _____ (*insert current crisis*).
But all my clever programming amounted
to mush in the mouth of a spoiled baby.

So I whined
"Who's to gain upstairs
from my basement failures?
Where's the glory stored
if I keep going out of business?
How's it good on You, Creator God,
that your premium-series species
drops the ball from a cloud so high
that, in terms of consequences,
it might as well have been an asteroid?

More answers, again too ample
for easy noting:
        "Get over you!
Better yet, get over '*Me*'!"
That mountainous "M"
is treacherous to pass
and the Pac-Man "e"
will eat everything
until trapped at last
by inmate ghosts
that consume it loudly.
Poor, poor Me.

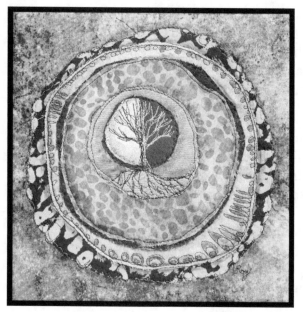

Day/Night #2

∽ Psalm 30 (b) ⌒

Lord, when I look at the balance of my faith,
it's clear that I'm in the black.
Born was I in abysmal debt
owing long before knowing.
But you've paid it off
and have taught me to live
richly within my means.

Give thanks to the Lord.
Employ her financial services.
The books she keeps are impeccable.
They show incomes you never
dreamed you had
and free you from all sorts
of extraneous expenditures.

I said to myself, "Now I can invest!"
and tried to handle my own portfolio,
but the dividends were slight to none.

My deepest business began sinking,
so I called out to You, my planner,
"What good will another bankruptcy
do for the innermost economy?
What can a washed-up soul pay back?
I believe," I cried,
"help manage my unbelief."
You changed my investment strategy
and helped me redefine profit.
Suddenly I draw abundance.
Thus I praise you all I can
and give your contact info
to every suit I meet.

∽ Psalm 31 ⌒

The acid rain of my broken marriage;
the climate change of my dying mother;
the famine of my downsized job…
global collides with local
in the crippled biosphere of my existence
where all major life systems are failing.

My refuge, my strength, my rock, my fortress,
my Superman, my James Bond, my NATO,
my Greenpeace, my pension, my health insurance,
my first-world-nation passport…
Don't knock down the walls on which I'm leaning.
Don't pull out the chair on which I'm about to sit.
It's a dirty joke, the junk we've made of the planet;
my personal scene is no less obscene.
Restore the wooded banks of my emotive rivers.
Remove the invasive species from my mind.
Halt the erosion that year by year
makes a dustbowl of my happiness.
My faith in you, once strong, has developed
respiratory conditions.
Will it ever run again?

Climate deniers mock my flooded home,
their laughter a thoughtless hurricane
lashing the poverty of my control.
I'm scared to death of having to adapt

to life up to my chest
in water mixed with sewage.

You are merciful and kind
of incomprehensible.
There's no telling what's next.
You've kept me going this far,
but I'm too frightened to watch the news.
Yet still I hope
and hope still more
that hope is more than merely habit.

 Psalm 32

A clean conscience is a hot cup of tea;
its soothing steam melts the outside storms
and when honey gets stirred in
sweetness permeates the calm.

But I have burned my inner works
gulping down too fast what should
be sipped with the care
of great discovery.

Mindlessness, ego, fear…
all these I confess.
Often I wash very attentively
the outside of the cup
forgetting the old leaves
that rot clumped in its bottom.

But grace alights on practice
like a dove on my eavestrough;
its nostalgic cooing
revives me,
reminds me
I was formed for peace.

Instruction. Teaching.
A wisdom wide to follow
plus a watchful hand
wealthy with gentle holy gestures
all point out a path
of steady surrender
mile after mile
until the stillest movement begins.

 **Psalm 33**

Take your time in tuning,
all you who charm music out
of wood, steel and air;
perfect pitch has our God
and an ear that breathes deep harmonies.
If you play, she'll provide the words;
her lyrics are (you could have guessed)
lyrical, they smell of rain-soaked earth.

Words that sing stars into being
and before them the sky they kiss;
words that say everything at once
in a timeless expression
unfolding dizzily like rasgueados
on a flamenco guitar.

A song that the musical and the wise
make their anthem,
so that wherever there is voice,
even in blues and mournful ballads,
there sings God.

Not science, not technology, not politics, not bureaucracy,
not doctrine, not free markets, not higher education, not
supreme courts
but Godly music—
that's what really saves.
So sing it.
Let your lives be sung.
Strike a wide-open chord
on your heartstrings
as your body reverberates
the blessings.

Psalm 34

A waterfall of blessings
immune to drought and dams
pours out of and over me.
May its mist moisten
all camera-eyed lookers-on.

And if their sighing of your Name
adds thunder to the wet,
we'll simply call it praise.

I googled God
and his mercy jumped off the screen.
You know, I felt so free
that I promptly closed all insistent Windows,
shut down my escape devices,
and went for a long, aimless walk
smack dab in the middle of the workday.

Taste and see the goodness of the Lord.
Breathe a little more slowly.
Feel the warmth of the coffee
you slug back.
Gently ask:
What is it I really like about its flavour?

Come, my children, take a look
at this sun-flecked wall
and tell me if the world

ain't just plain old stunning?
Once you answer then just keep silent
a spell and listen
to the truth dance its echo
in your heart's empty tomb.

With God there's so much soft-eyed
deep seeing,
there's hearing of motherly power.
Why would you ever want to try
to hide yourself from this attention?

For every minute of distraction
there's an hour of what-a-pleasure-to-be-here presence.
Taste and see the goodness of the Lord.
Smile as you constantly return
circling the still point.
Be kind
and remember
you're pretty much paid
according to your compassion.

∽ Psalm 35 ◡

Look how the books have all been cooked
against us.
The Law, in wig and powder,
covers a sneering, bearded face
as ugly as sin

and as partial.
Mothers, don't let your sons grow up
to be assholes.

Smash the glass ceiling that checks
a woman's ascension.
Put wrecking ball to wall of every
home built a female prison.
Stop the clock before happy hour,
when impunity buddies with abuse.
Cut the lights!
Kill the power!
Turn out the bully drunks.
Let every girl proudly hang
around her neck the sign
"OUT OF SERVICE".
Proudly and loudly
the red-robed chorus sings
"The tragedy is over."

From these many galaxies
in my ovaries
a cry of living victory
will right these lopsided societies.

False witnesses; fake science; bad faith
all make a crackpot case
against us.
Why is the "fairer" sex
official subject to injustice?
Who does not owe his all to woman?

And yet the debt
is thrown back
in her face to pay!

Bullshit! Enough
half-baked housewife mythology.
Enough little-man complex
swaggering around lost in
the ten-gallon hat of a divine Patriarch.
We don't want tables turned
but tables shared,
both in the eating and in the cleaning.

God! To think it's taken this long
and will take longer still.
It's a rotten joke gone putrid
in the ageless telling:
Catcalls, entitled eyes, indecent hands
and the perennial deep-rooted weed
of dismissal are the unruliness
of our daily garden.
God
the transcendent
the transgendered
the transformative
force with your shoulder
put to the wheel of culture;
give a little push…
a little more…
roll away the stone…
let the entombed arise

and victory will be sung
by all the living
now joyfully released
from phony fears
of what they might have stood to lose.

 Psalm 36

Monsanto owns the seeds.
Remington sells the guns.
The churches vow silence.

Institutions/Corporations
drunk, abusive giants
too big for their britches
saving their own flaky skins
with crude weapons
carved out of poor-person bones.
No single sleeper's dreams
harbour their entire harm;
evil is more widely distributed.

Small is beautiful,
the local lovely;
these little molehills of daily quiet life
are like splendid mountains
to the shining eye
wise enough to see.

how invaluable the compassion
born of communities
that care, that stare long
into the fires of adversity
and watch dance
flames of solidarity.

a river cleaned
a park protected
elder trees respected
for their sagacity
pesticidal public enemies reformed,
brought into the fold
of those living well within their means
of common householding;
the waterwheel revolution
turning on a smile to the tune
of the freely running stream.

let me move within the movement
let me take my loving turn
showing my back to those institutions
that spend so much on full
frontal attacks.

∽ Psalm 37 ∾

This is one of the longer ones
and reads (forgive my eyes)
like a lengthy list of wish fulfillments.
#37: three & seven
two good-luck digits
pointing to perfection
and summing up the Law.

Chorus:
The blessed will the Earth possess;
the wicked are simply poison.

Think positive.
Visualize your win.
Avoid all self-defeating language.
Imitate successful people,
except where they go wrong.
Generally, it's good to be yourself,
provided that your self is generally good.

Chorus

The cynic is just a saint with blisters:
one mile too many in shoes too small.
As long as she doesn't litter,
her passing little harms the view.
All kinds of gaits and strides
fit within this camino.

Chorus

The blowhards are also here today
and tomorrow gone.
Once there were plenty of fair-sized trees
for them to stir in,
now there's nary a leafy limb left.

Chorus

Good & bad just seems too easy:
a binary code that can't compute
in a world of bugs, viruses and dissociative weather
stomping towards a rainless flood.

All the same, in the age of *climax change*,
something remains of the old religion.
The remnant, faithful to the coming cooing of a dove,
clings to the twig of laurel like a lifeline
as the waters rise.

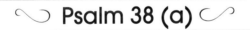

Psalm 38 (a)

Is it rage divine destroying me?
Diabetes, heart disease, obesity, depression, early-onset
Alzheimer's, insomnia,
and every shape and shade of cancer listed
in the corporeal catalogue.
Not a single cell in my body

has dodged the bullet of your ire,
inflamed by habits of my living.

Bad decisions, corporate and personal,
come crashing down upon my head…
who knew convenience was such a killer?

Saturated fats, sedentarism, high-fructose corn syrup,
hyper-refined flour,
seas of hand sanitizer, screens,
screens, and more screens,
even electric lights
that everywhere echo your brightness, God,
have drained my melatonin and taken
to dismantling me.
I hardly move
and the few parts that do
get stung by the killer-bees
of carpal tunnel syndrome.

Just about everybody feels the same,
but no one cares about the rest;
to support groups we go
to certify that mine isn't
the most hopeless of all cases,
at least there are others fatter, dumber and more distraught
than me.

As for you, O God, I pray
when the drugs don't work
or the power fails

or some celebrity tells me to
on daytime talk-show television.
I used to go to church.
My parents took us.
It was boring and the pews were hard.

I was promised more than this
and got everything that wasn't mentioned.
I used to joke that the Coca-Cola Corporation
owned copyright on 65% of my body.
It isn't funny anymore.

Don't leave me, Lord.
I don't know you yet.
I simply bought what was advertised
and didn't think…

to question.

 Psalm 38 (b)

Creator, don't pay me back in kind.
Please do not do unto me as I,
against my holy hopes,
have been prone to do to others.

There isn't a pristine inch remaining to my forest;
slash and burn are the prints left by my gold-spurred boots.

The sins of my living are alive
in the death of what sustains me.
Plastic oozes from my pores;
my body bends unthinking beneath the weight
it burdens gentle Earth with.

I feel a piercing in my back—
it's the stare of coming generations.
Dreadfully I sleep
knowing my dreams are minutely being watched.

God, you're party to my fears.
I don't swallow a single sigh
for this land deprived of care.
My complicity sickens me;
putrid my recurring excuses.

My partners in co-evolution
flee me like the plague;
we grew up together
and the hard truths they hurl at me
I duck as if they were lies.

Deaf, blind and asinine,
I ramrod forward,
loading the musket aimed
squarely in my face.

But I hope in you, Creator,
that you make, if not good,
then at least a little better
this deep-down longing

which so often stops short
by doing bad.

Green blood is on my hands.
Too clearly I see it.
Too easily do I put on pretty gloves.
Indifference can overpower me.
Convenience can sweep clean in,
the mighty conquistador.

Creator, don't leave us orphan,
Mother Earth and me.
Come quickly and pluck us
from the water I keep putting
on to boil.

 **Psalm 39**

I said to myself, *"That's it! I'm through!*
I'll never talk politics with this meat-headed crew
again. I'll bite my tongue and go mum,
or at very most deafly hum."
But from bad it just got worse.
The whole country went south.

Heartburn from greasy laws,
blood pressured from the uphill run,
panting until suddenly the steam whistle blows,
the coronary pops
and my ancient inner-child disappointment bawls:

"I can't do this anymore!
I want to die right here and now!"

A breath, a breeze, a murmur in the trees
is all our blimp of an ego is,
a bit of trapped hot air
casting a high altitude, self-congratulatory
shadow willfully mistaken as fame.

Hope? Where's that on the map?
Just east of the Kingdom
of Oz.
Still I circle it in fluorescent yellow
as my destination.
These real-life swamps I slog through in real time…
please put them all right next to that highlighted ring.
Remind me I'm nothing.
Convince me I'm loved.
I constantly forget the first
and have never really got the second.
Ignorance is blis-
ters poorly covered with Band-Aids
that my endless walking savagely pulls off.

Mozart's Starling

∽ Psalm 40 ∾

Waiting with everything I got
(down now to a plastic shopping bag)
waiting for the coyote call
that snarls in whispers "*hurry*,"
I'm getting out
of a homeland turned cesspool
where not a square foot
of solid rock remains to stand on.

"Refugee" is my mouth's new song,
equal parts curse and promise.
It's the lament women wail
beside a mangled family.
It's the hit song that plays in every head
slipping across the border.
Many a marvel come-from-heaven
have sent me forward up till now,
much like a stone kicked along
between the feet of a few idle boys
going to good-for-nothing nowhere.

Everything I've lost is a clearing house of sorrow.
"Sacrifice" is the name they use
when they tell me it's my turn to cross.
"Will" sounds like a wall impossible to climb.
"Maybe", "perhaps", "with any luck"
ring more true
but obviously less beautiful.

From the fragments of my new-lost life
I puzzle for an answer
in the immensity of pain
boiling over down my pot of faith.
I believed it all beyond me:
the whirlwind of war and hate and scarcity
that flattens my place of birth.

Lord, give me a deeper clue.
I can't do this crucifixion crossword.
It makes no sense;
the verticals and horizontals
leave me in a state of such tortured confusion
that often I feel right back at home.
If human, why are we treated like mountains,
told forcefully to pick ourselves up
and be hurled into the sea?

 **Psalm 41**

Happy the little piggy that stops
on the way to market
to lift a painted turtle off the road.
The Lord will knock on her heart's door
with a bouquet of flowers
and after speaking briefly with his eyes
will enter there
where the two will fall in love
seated at the kitchen table.

Said the little piggy: *Mercy!*
I have been so consumed with eating well,
with building my brick mansions.
The Market was my temple
eight days a week.
I have walk-in closets, storage lockers
and offshore accounts all to save my bacon.

The night-time teeth-grinding, semi-sleeping voices
would off and on whistle:
"Geez! She's sick to death of getting ahead.
It's a terminal case of Self."

Even my inner broker would sometimes
tsk, tsk me
shaking his head.

But you, Lordly lover, please kiss
the pennies off my eyes.
Put meadows on my way to market
and help me lose myself in them.
Protect me from the abattoir
of my own avarice,
from the butcher of my greed.
You make me happy
in my home of sticks.
Hear them clack together
your praise forever.
Amen.

Psalm 42

As a deer in shrinking habitat
longs for flowing streams
now diverted into culverts
aimed at cotton fields,
so my soul longs for you,
O orphaned God,
abandoned in the cradle
of your creation.

As a polar bear on the thawing ice floe
starves for colder days
and fatter seals,
so my soul starves for you,
O God of drawn-out second comings
and diminishing returns.

When will I not have to see your face,
O Lord, bruised and swollen in the earth?
I grind my teeth in my sleep
because the grief far outsizes
my consciousness, which spins
wheels in the muddy evidence
of your non-existence.

These things haunt my mind
as it leaks out across the keyboard:
    the streams my grandparents
      drank straight out of:

the routed glaciers;
the raped woods;
the elephants, pandas, gorillas, coral reefs
bald eagles, monarch butterflies;
all victims of their own beauty,
destroyed on stage by the clutching
hands of crazed fans.

No wonder you are anxious
and autistic, my soul;
this emptying earth is too much
to live on.
Speak to God!
Do not choke closed!

My soul is not high functioning;
it slinks towards corners, screens
and private language.
Therefore, I must remember
former pain and mass extinctions
and trust that creation is a game
without a final level,
without a highest score.

I say to my creator,
don't throw in the towel.
Keep the miracle factory open.
Step up the output
of beauty and diversity.
Advertise well.

No wonder you are anxious
and autistic, my soul,
the emptying earth is too much
to live on.
Weep. Scream. Plead with God.
Do not choke closed.

Psalm 43

Do us justice, O God,
defend the cause of the unborn,
we who dwell
in the New World of existence
already colonized by the living
trash and greed of our
stiff-necked ancestors.

How can you, Creator,
countenance such desecration?
Why are we damned
before we start,
sentenced to a desert
repellant to our birth?
Send your truth and your light
as midwives.
Give us a common home
where to be born;
common: as in shared,
as in simple, as in normal
in the longer arc of history.

Why should we be damned
before we start,
sentenced to a desert
repellant to our birth?

Trust in God, please do,
all you children
already dying to come.

Psalm 44

God, we've watched the documentaries,
and our grandparents, when little we see them,
have told and retold patched-knee stories
of how it was back in the day of Nature.
How afternoons would bleed
into endless evenings of Out-of-Doors,
staunched only at last by the black bandages
of night wrapped firmly round the fading red
of late summer sunsets.
How street hockey, hide-and-seek
and capture the flag were the democratically
elected, power-to-the-people sports
before the parental coup d'état
that put a dictator in the driver's
seat of the armoured car forever
transferring minor political prisoners
from field to rink to swimming pool
and other gulags of developmental excellence.

How the ravine behind the back fence
was a reality apart, more fantastical
than any virtual mask.
How the trees and mud and vines
and bruises made one single body,
ecstatic, wild and irrepressible.

Where are we now? Allergic, asthmatic,
autistic, controlled by an overweening love
afraid to shut off the suckling spigot.
Children of a litigious creed
that believes every scraped knee
tears open on the maleficence
of some odious stranger, whose perversion
must pay back one hundredfold.
Liberty is the stuff of dreams;
forests are found thinly sliced
in the occasional books we briefly handle;
an illicit lot with weeds and anthills
and maybe—glory be!—a praying mantis
is a faraway third world feature—
sad, too sad but true.
So babied have we been that now
we're butter left out on a hot day:
easily spread too thin.

All this but we're still children
born to and for discovery,
loaded springs of learning
in dire need of woods and streams
to catch our fast uncoiling.

Made to play, we're forced to wait
until the protective plastic
and professional supervision
are securely in place.
By then it's time to round up marks
and trophies in order to grow
more gainfully employed than our friends,
better known as our competitors.
Hello? What's going on? Get on it, God,
before the whole thing's gone.
We're just a bunch of kids.
And Childhood, in case you haven't noticed,
is way up high on the endangered species list.

 Psalm 45

Picture this, what's inside my head
aching to flow out through my pen:
    a person of power
    laurelled with grace
    whose words assure our eyes
    with truly gentle watercolours.

The weapon of good persuasion
is the ploughshare strapped to her waist.
Victory is the wind in her hair
blowing off the sea of justice.
The beach beneath her feet is clean;
the handsome ocean with carnival-life teams.

God is behind her
who is beyond woman or man:
pure humanity in a body
disciplined by wisdom
and not afraid of aging.

Dispensable all luxuries of beauty:
the creams, powders and perfumes.
The industry can't touch the person
I picture, light years away
from consumptive shadows of self.

She's the king I vote for,
the lord we must all elect.
Hers the creative government of the people
in grateful service to the Earth.
Monarchy is by no means dead.
We simply have not prayed enough to choose it.

 **Psalm 46**

How on Earth do we square them:
a faith in creative goodness
and the acidic evidence
that Creation is thoroughly screwed?
Beneath the rainbow covenant
that stretches like fallout
over the post-diluvial world
sea levels, like maggots, creep up

reversing by inches the Genesis timeline,
sending old Noah nervously back to his toolshed.
The City of God, is it sustainable?
Does it sit too heavily on the fields
and flowers of the Promised Land?
Are its citizens oily slickers
who can't tell an elm tree from an oak?

Still, our Creator lives
and we are the living proof
even in our decadence.

Come and see the Wonders of the World,
and I don't mean the pyramids
or Machu Picchu.
Get out of the plane and onto the ground
bend down
and study a square foot of forgotten earth.
There's mundane magic most marvellous
moving around:
living proof our Creator lives
despite our slow-motion, repeat-loop
Fall.

Psalm 47

Plato said "Democracy stinks!
Only not quite as bad as dictatorship!"
so I vote for You, O God,

and Your ever new
Enlightened Monarch Movement

Well aware am I how
Church and State must separate
like oil and vinegar
thank goodness you're neither
this nor that
Your platform gets me thinking
outside the leaky ballot box

at rallies and conventions we sing
at ribbon cuttings and townhalls we sing
in my hidden heart I wear your button
on my inner lawn is firmly planted
Your crisp campaign sign: GOD RULES!

Left and Right unite!
Liberals and Conservatives, go on
pucker up and kiss!
Sweeping this election,
may You clean out the icky cobwebs
of our chronic democratic discontent.

 **Psalm 48**

God is grate
and sewer,
often overwhelmed by these

new-fashioned floods taking streets
as the flash-storm blitzkrieg
rains fury upon the city.
No cerebrum calculated just how quickly
growth would outstrip
sacred infrastructure.

Condominiums on every corner
carve canyons seldom plumbed by sun,
and the ant-farm populace
observing itself through glass
scarcely summons curiosity
much less the will to comprehend.

O City of God!
O noise and power!
All your holy temples
are now rezoned for commercial use.

We meditate in subways, elevators,
single-occupant vehicles
staring straight ahead
self-enclosed
spiritually above eye contact
and other human forms
of undisciplined distraction.

Take a look around
but do it furtively.
Don't let anyone catch you searching.
God is everywhere, see?

But mostly very early
sweeping streets
before you join the regiment
rushing lockstep to work.

 Psalm 49

So you're rich?
Big deal!
Although your marble mausoleum
has the capacity to house
an entire living family
from Honduras,
you, when dead and nothing,
will find it awful tight.

So you're handsome?
Lah-di-dah!
Have you ever seen tattoos
on old-man arms
dirty blue and misshapen
that boasted proud stories
when the colours were still clear?
Gradually no one listens
and those petroglyphs grow
inscrutable
faded and ridiculous.

So you're beautiful?

YAWN!
Just like all the other cosmetic queens
now manicured by worms.
As the world turns,
those dizzy with power
fall to the same earth
as those who never got
their prostration off the ground.

So chirp away.
Feather your nest.
Lay your golden eggs.
But sure as Sunday
there'll come an afternoon
when your entire Me-Empire
will be no more
than a pot of boiled chicken
and an omelette overcooked.
So don't compete,
don't covet,
don't grovel,
not even with yourself.
Love what you've been given
and smile as you kindly pass it on.
We'll all meet on the other side,
soft and naked
as clouds in heaven.

Beethoven's Pastoral

 Psalm 50

The special effects? Out of this world!
    God in the tornado!
    God in the hurricane!
    God in the volcano!
Even the rolling credits
gobsmack a twice-turned cheek.

But before the budget's blown
they shoot all those stiller scenes
predestined not to make the cut,
yet haunting all the same:
stories dead and never buried.

God thunders:
    Get off your conspiracy theologies!
    Look me in the eye
    and tell me straight
    if I have cancer.
    It ain't your tiptoeing I desire,
    nor your tulips
    but your fidelity to the body
    I have danced in
    all these ages.
    I have died more times
    than there are stars you cannot see
    in outward-rushing, raging galaxies
    blotted out by your motion-sensing porch lights.
    Not your sympathy,

nor your science,
only your simplicity
of heart... this the sacrifice
I ask of you, eternal teenagers
too cool for hand-me-down belief.

As for sin,
you've already had enough
said and disregarded.
Your VISA card has been charged.
Worry about the interest on any late payments.

There's a love around here lurking.
Get involved.
Every time you find yourself
on a site of conspiracy theology,
pack up your tent and leave.

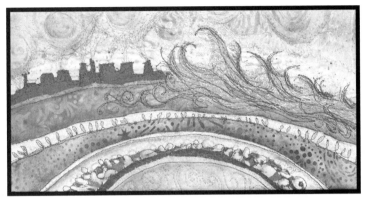

Antibody

Kindled by an early love of hand embroidery, Lorraine Roy's techniques permit her to 'paint' with fabric and thread using a sewing machine. All her work explores connections between art, science and nature. Most of her imagery is inspired by the biology, mythology and cultural impact of trees, classic symbols of our connection with the natural world. She continues to acquire new knowledge and insights about them in order to better address and convey our mutual rich and complex kinship.